One in Soul Imprints

*Pearls, Rubies,
and Diamonds of the Heart*

IANA LAHI

One in Soul Imprints

Published through Spirit Gateways® Publishing
All Rights Reserved
Copyright © 2020 by IANA LAHI

Interior Book Design and Layout by:
www.integrativeink.com

ISBN: 978-0-9862384-8-2

Library of Congress Number: 2020916577

No part of this publication may be reproduced, stored in a retrieval system, or transmitted in any form or by any means electronic, mechanical, photocopying, recording or otherwise, without the written permission of the author or publisher.

Gems of Wisdom From:

BE: The Humanity Blueprint Volume I
One in Soul

**Dedicated To The
Light Within
You.**

BE ONE. BE YOU.®

To listen authentically, you must slow everything down inside your mind by listening for the *space between* sounds, words, thoughts, and your breath in your body.

To suspend your beliefs *and* to suspend disbelief, you must be ready to receive.

When you listen to and embrace the calling of your soul, there is a spark of recognition that you are more than the thoughts you have, the emotions that run you, or your physical challenges. You begin to realize your limitless possibility, and the fears and dramas of your life dissolve.

By denying the existence of our soul, we as individuals and as a world collective have excommunicated from the part of ourselves that is God. For it is through the soul that the longing to know God, and to open to the love that is beyond all suffering is found.

The purpose of your life is to know, express,
and complete your soul, and experience
its connection with Infinite Source.

Most souls choose before coming into a lifetime if they will work with their soul truths and lessons or not. A soul chooses a new family that will assist it to heal whatever fragmentary baggage it is carrying. Whether through positive or negative experiences, a soul will face the belief structures, and emotional and spiritual patterns that must be addressed in order to find Oneness with Infinite Source.

The light that lives in your heart awakens by reconnecting, rebuilding, and restructuring your soul's truth and essence.

The soul exists beyond time and space, and is a multidimensional consciousness.

Every aspect of your soul matters.
Your natural state is to be whole, and it is important
to get that despite what rationalizations may
arise, no aspect of yourself can be left behind. The
infinite intelligence of Source works through you to
guide you to seek all of the parts of your God Self.
Once reconnected, you and God can BE One.

Fear is just a thought, a perception created from the mind believing it is the center of its own existence.

Joy is a state of being where you are able to soak in and BE with the perfection of what is.

Each time that you practice BEing in the essence of your truth and True Self, you build momentum and fill your inner energetic fuel tank. When life's difficulties strike, the reservoir of your awakened energies will get you through your life challenge. Even in the most difficult moments, embrace the love that you are, and become the love.

How you accept the IS that is you, and what you do with it *is* what makes your life whole. The love that you open into for yourself and for others begins to remove the separations that you have created over time. As you hear, feel, see, and know your True Self, the anger, hurt, sorrows and pain that were created by living in separation can dissolve, and the love that you are can emerge.

Anytime that you have had your power taken from you or you have given it away, you have the choice to practice compassion for yourself and hold a big space of acceptance, and self forgiveness, or separate from love and step into shame. When you step into shame, anger follows. Whether you stuff it or express it, the anger can only be healed by embracing the original wound, and shift what you believe in the moment about yourself.

Awaiting in the subconscious of your body is a soul aspect bursting to love, a soul aspect ready to bring joy, a soul aspect waiting to explode your creativity wide open, and one that will connect you to your Higher Self, and when unified, exudes the essence of your Original Self. Trust the power of light that is ignited as your awakened soul merges with the pure BEingness of Infinite Source.

The power of the love within you is so strong that the universe will do anything it can to have you surrender to its ultimate truth.

Bringing the light of your heart into every aspect of your life will authenticate how you live your life. The truth of your God Self will reveal itself to you as the light. Your power source shifts from being aligned to the lower aspects of your mind to the higher aspects of your mind. The energetic shifts into BEing the ISness of your light and power give you a new way of living in alignment with what will never fail you or let you down. You are given the keys to move from fear, doubt, self-rejection, judgment and suffering into love, freedom, truth, wisdom and compassion.

Your love is a flame.
Your love is warm tender and roaring fire of light communion with sacred truth. Who are you within the borders of your heart? Can you feel its essence burning, surging, touching, holding, pushing away, fragile, listless, aching, wanting? Can you know its flame? You are that. All that you are is the golden embodied flame of Oneness that exists within you. BE within the earth of yourself, the water of your well, the air of your breath, the fire of your passion and the etheric expansion of your infinite nature. May these elements give you serenity, comfort and peace.

When you surrender to love, you become One with life because you are living from the original essence that you truly are. As you practice filling yourself in love you are fulfilling what you came here for. How to love yourself is the ultimate lesson and enables you to love the world and BE in service to the world.

Love is the root. Love is the true power.
It is the foundation of all things.

You must lead your life from the integrated center of your heart, Spirit and soul rather than solely from your mind.

Your divine truth — your soul's essence, are the nectar of healing and rejuvenation in every cell in your body. The universe and you become One as the molecules of thoughts, feelings, and energies emerge and bloom from the seeds of your soul. There is no going back once you walk through the doorway of your awakening heart. What awaits you is a torrential ongoing wave of divine guidance, support, and love that vaporizes your past, clears your wounds, unlocks the gates to heaven and reminds you in every moment that you are an incarnated holy and whole precious spark of God Infinite Source.

Give yourself permission to BE creative with each moment. BE willing to go beyond what your mind is saying and to love the essence of who you are, rather than what you think you are and what you have or do not have on the external. Find the bliss of BEING the essence of *who you are*.

Your soul will always move toward the light.
It may meditate, emote, create, love, or explore
itself through the arts, love, God, or nature. It may
choose to seek what it has lost through new life
experiences that touch into disempowered parts of
it that are waiting to be found. Your light is deep
inside of your soul and it is the wayshower and guide
leading you back to Original Source energy.

True prosperity is born through recognizing and knowing what and who you really are, and it can take the place of lack, emptiness, remorse, self-judgment, fear and pain. As you embody the pure light of truth to radiate and fill your Whole Self you become a magnet for prosperity. The gates of the kingdom open within you, revealing God's love, and eternal freedom. The truth of yourself does set you free to BE.

The divine will speak through your heart and soul's expansion. Even at times when your heart begins to shut down, nurture it with tenderness, and open to the light in your heart beyond what your mind can perceive. Listen to the song of your soul.

As the soul awakens, it will come to realize that the only way to *BE complete* is through itself. When you love another it will come from an overflowing wellspring created by being sourced from within yourself. Your relationships will be created and sustained through sharing the joy that you are rather than trying to be filled up by another. You will feel One unto yourself.

When your soul unites with your heart there is a moment of realizing that you can choose the wholeness of your soul over your ego.

Think of your soul as the artistic, creative, healing, intuitive, insightful and knowing part of your Self. When you quiet your mind, you are making it safe for your soul to emerge and "talk." Your soul will guide you to expand, to trust and to listen through its ears, and to see through its eyes.

When past pain, suffering and attachments are embraced by the joy within our heart, the courage to release the past can blossom. Within even the most wounded heart exists joy and its light has the power to illuminate even the most painful past experiences.

How you hold on, hold back, and hold in transform as you open your heart to the truth of your divine essence found through clearing your sanskaras—the imprints and impressions carried into this lifetime and created in your early childhood in this present lifetime.

When your soul is whole, you can release your mind from its duty of being in control. It will hang on to control until your full power is restored. Your full power is restored once your soul knows that it is ONE with Source, living in its full light, and can trust the love within itself.

Your soul is not just the spark of your life, it is also the catalyst and gateway that makes it possible to BE ONE in yourself and with all of life. There is no escaping the soul or its call.

Joy teaches you to let go of what you think you need to be and do, and all the ways that you block love from coming into your life. Joy teaches you to get out of the way and to just BE. Joy teaches you how to receive support from the universe. Once you open to receive help and support from the universe joy can flow in through the door you have opened.

No matter how sad, hurt, angry, lost or confused an emotion may feel, beneath it exists the authentic presence and voice of your True Self.

The more you yearn for joy, the more you must release and let go of the attachments that you have created to the role that you play in the world, your own identity, and what you believe you need to be to get what you want. From a place of BEing empty and receptive, life can begin to fill the goblet of your heart.

Underneath all of the inner sorrow, pain or fear that you hide behind or use as a barrier to living fully lives the essence of your True Self.

Joy stabilizes both the integrity of love and truth within your soul, and ultimately pulls you into union with the divine. By trusting your joy you will come through even the most challenging moments and circumstances of your life.

Each of us has a Core Emotional Wound that is the gateway to our soul's karmic completion.

Your ego is a false Self that is created by you when you feel that who you are is not enough, and incapable of fulfilling the expectations being placed upon you. Your ego Self steps up as your True Self goes into hiding in your base energy centers. Your ego Self comes into existence to help you handle the inner pain created by feeling abandoned, betrayed or rejected ABR'd) . Rather than staying in your light, you shift into fear, and separation, and in a split second your ego is created from the depths of your subconscious and survival nature.

The moment-to-moment experiences of your life, those that both make and break you, serve as the building blocks and doorway to your deeper Self and truth.

The soul aspects that you leave behind always contain your spiritual power. The loss of your spiritual power ends up translating in a perceived loss of your personal power and human potential.

Remember to BE present and to listen to the inner voice and frequency of your soul. The more that you stay with yourself, the more you will be able to feel and receive the unconditional love that lives within you. Unconditional love lives in every cell of your body and drives your soul forward to meet and merge with the divine. The light of Spirit unlocks a deep knowingness within your cells. Discover and embrace the love within you by bringing together your soul aspects with unconditional acceptance.

Life itself is the experience of your soul expanding and contracting to evolve. We are all given opportunities to grow through the smallest and most difficult challenges of our lives with mastery. The union that is possible with your mind, heart, body and Spirit creates the opportunity for your soul to experience your original, divine love, and Oneness with Infinite Source.

Each time that you allow the spiritual essence of your
True Self to fill your spine, heart center, and soul,
you are creating a new connection to God and a new
structure to allow for the transcendence and release
of your impressions, sanskaras, and egoic mind.

Within you there is a SELF that is ONE in God.
It is the light and truth of your Whole Self unified.
It knows and remembers the promise of ONENESS,
and will guide you forward if you allow it to.

Your soul is a fire of passion, clarity,
determination, and peace that fuels the evolution
of your BEing into its true destiny.

Duality is the maze that we move through to discover that who we really are, are BEings who live in a perpetual state of Oneness. When we live from the state of Oneness, we do not care what color a persons skin is, what religion they follow, what nationality they are born into or how much money they make a year. We do not separate love and hate within our subconscious through judgment. We have learned to embrace what we hate about our self, choose to change it and nurture what we love about our self. When we embrace both sides of duality and accept their oppositional nature, we find a point of neutrality. This point of neutrality is a gateway through duality and into the union of our divine and human natures.

Always remember that your soul, and in fact your entire BEing, is one, big, highly charged consciousness of light. You are a body of vibrating photons of charged light connecting in every moment. If you could see your true energetic Self, you would see yourself as waves of light flowing like the ocean expanding and contracting in the universe. This is both a physical and spiritual truth.

Part of stepping into *BEing conscious* involves becoming aware of our true divine feminine and masculine energies verses what we have known and adopted as our societal masculine and feminine selves. We must come to recognize that there is fine line between carrying on the chosen traditions and behaviors of our families that are based upon both unconditional and conditional love, and the habits and behaviors that we carry on through denial, control and disconnection from the Self.

When you experience joy in your life, it opens you to love. The greater the joy that you choose to BE in, the deeper the love you can find within yourself and others. If you find it difficult to find joy in your life, first seek the peace that comes from being real with what hurts inside yourself. Peace will bring you joy because joy is a state of BEing where conflict does not exist. Once inner pain is recognized, acknowledged and accepted, the joy of your soul will guide you through any conflict.

The divine feminine is raw power. **IT IS YOUR POWER**.
Your divine feminine is creation centered, knowing, certain, bold, fearless, expansive, receptive, trailblazing, ferocious, directive, empowering, perceptive, passionate, nurturing, intuitive, life-giving, unlimitedly creative, visionary, assertive, allowing, wise, telepathic, and receiving.
Your divine feminine connects you into pure creation energy—the void where all creative and life giving energies originate from.

Your divine masculine expresses as love. **IT IS YOUR LOVE.**
Your divine masculine is unconditional love. It is embracing, compassionate, dynamic, gentle, patient, action-oriented, building, sustaining, steadfast, goal-centered, structuring, shaping, propelling, accepting, unifying, consistent, discerning, exploring, determined, designing, and accountable.
Your divine masculine contains essential life sustaining and supporting qualities that enable you to flourish and accomplish your goals, soul mission and life's purpose.

Without the connection with the internal divine feminine, the societal masculine has become a slave to the external forces of greed and corruption. Without a connection to the divine feminine a constant nagging to fill the body, mind and spirit with more and more thoughts, stuff and fluff is creating a world culture of internal emptiness. Both men and women who have disconnected from their divine feminine have lost the ability to embody their healthy power and to fulfill the higher calling of their soul in this lifetime while in service to the greater good of humanity.

Your integrated divine masculine and feminine energies are your spiritual power. The divine masculine intelligence naturally grows and supports life instead of destroying it. However, the human masculine has been forced throughout history to withstand the corruption of cultural, religious and political institutions and roles that have been created through living in separation and denial from divine masculine and feminine integration. The desecration of our divine masculine and feminine soul energies was the harbinger for all future spiritual and human violations to come.

The divine feminine initiates total transformation of our deep-seated patterns that hold the false masculine within each of us in place. For it is within the total integration of our divine masculine and feminine energies that our higher purpose is revealed, activated and implemented.

The divine feminine energies move into your body through the earth gateways and the divine masculine energies move into your body through the heavenly gateways.

Their union in the center of your heart is a powerful initiation on your soul awakening path and being *One in Soul.* Therefore, all of your *Power Point Centers,* and specifically your lower centers, must be engaged in your soul reconnection.

The divine feminine opens your direct access to Infinite Source and provides instantaneous direct knowledge and understanding of your true purpose. You become tapped into a power that never fails you and helps you to heal yourself and others just by shifting your focus. The divine feminine is the healer of the body. She has courage and clarity that once integrated directs life to recreate circuits and channels of power that are destined to heal our world.

Within the abundance found within the integration of our divine masculine and feminine consciousness we are able to live the lives we are born to live. Our divine and liberated masculine presence must teach and liberate the socialized and imprisoned inner masculine energies within us all so that we learn how to emulate a new way of BEing ONE. The old paradigm of socialized masculine energies has taught us how to close the heart for the sake of accomplishment, and neglect and abandon our creative forces. It teaches us to reject our spiritual truth and remain attached to family and societal values that use and abuse the clarity, wisdom and new power found within the heart. The divine masculine must be valued as deeply as we honor and revere the divine feminine. Together they can and will shift our planet back into balance. It is up to each one of us to come into a new relationship with our internal and external divine masculine expression.

When you walk through the portal of your heart you activate a field of electromagnetic energies that also exist within the universe. Once you are activated as a unified light being the divine spectrum of the universe has the ability to move you in perfect alignment with the greater evolutionary molecular spin of your soul. In the center point within your heart is the treasure chest of profound love that you have always been and always will be.

The more that you let go of examining what is wrong with yourself and with your life and instead open to the light and love within yourself, the easier it will become to move forward on your life path and soul destiny.

Your true power is divine love that
has awakened in your soul.

When you truly surrender, you are receiving and empowering the part of your God Self that yearns to be seen, heard, received, and reconnected to.

The truth of who you are is found by clearing the cellular memories within your body and choosing to see, feel, and be in the divine truth of who you really are.

The depth of the split within your heart center
is what fuels all of your physical, emotional,
psychological and spiritual dilemmas and crises.

Your *Power Point Centers* began to
develop while you were in
utero, before birth. The development
of your *Power Point Centers*
is shaped by your past life spiritual
experiences, perceptions,
and attunement; the energies within
your mother's womb; and
the energies that you were born into within your family and
surrounding environment. How you
relate to yourself, Infinite
Source, and your environment creates imbalance or balance
within your Power Points and your Bodymind circuitry.

When your body, mind and soul are energetically separate and split off from the light of your God Self, you are unable to stay connected to your life path and what is best for you because your decision making process is disconnected to your whole intelligence.

All of the *Power Point Centers* contain the higher and lower aspects of the mind. They each serve a particular function of integrating the body and the mind, thus creating the BodyMind.

You will experience feeling whole as your divine masculine and feminine forces meet in your heart center and come together in union. This happens because your heart is the entryway into the love and power that makes up all of life. Your heart center, which is your true mind, is like a tuning fork that resonates to the thoughts and feelings of the universe.

As we walk through these challenging times on planet earth, we each have the opportunity to awaken and step out of the separations we individually create and live within.

Your soul aspect will show up as a version of you at the age when you last experienced being fully seen, heard or received. It may be the energy and presence of you as an infant, toddler, child or teenager. This part, when first discovered, may be angry, impatient, crying, happy, sad, withdrawn, hopeful, dynamic or lifeless. Don't be misled. These aspects of you hold the keys to your full power and potential as a human-spiritual being. The emotions are real, but they are not who you are. The parts of yourself that carry your spiritual power show themselves to you because your soul has a built in goal to be whole, and to feel One with itself and with God. The moment you unconditionally embrace your soul aspect while meditating and being within the light inside of you, you will begin to heal your relationship with your soul.

The power of the love within you is so strong
that the universe will do anything it can to
have you surrender to its ultimate truth.

The *One in Soul* experience begins the evolutionary process of bringing back together your divine and human nature into union.

We are never taught how to recognize the deeper feelings of sorrow, hurt or separation within us. It is often easier to split off from the light of our True Self and identify with the pain that manifests as resentment, anger, fear, or sadness. We let our ego take over as the great protector and soother of our fragmented Self so we can survive. These feelings can live on for years until we recognize how we empower our ego to sedate the pain and avoid being who we really are.

Your sanskaras are the imprints of time and experience, chiseled into your energetic bodies that, once realized and released, open waves of potentiality in your life. These grooves, scars, wounds, holes, caverns, wellsprings, and oceans of impressions carry all past experiences, beliefs, and emotions. They color how you perceive, respond, think, and make choices and will hold tight until the light of your God Self penetrates them and begins to transform them.

Your human nature must go through its evolution of
discovering both light and dark, separation and suffering,
being asleep and awakening, until the moment that
you move through the illusions of dualistic thinking.

To heal we need to accept the light within each soul aspect and reconnect their gifts into our heart. Our purest power waits in our darkest and most hidden soul part. As we accept our newfound power, we must commit to using it in the highest ways always.

By acknowledging and honoring yourself with love, it will become easier to let go of attachments you thought you needed to be happy. You will learn to
let go of things needing to
look a certain way. You may have an
image of how you want to
be in this lifetime, but sometimes it is
necessary to let go of that
image to advance forward. What you
really want to happen in
your life can happen once you release
your grip on how things
need to be to make you feel valued
and significant. As you allow
yourself to merge with your heart,
you realize that happiness
comes from being in the heart of your soul.

All of the ways that your wounded ego, and separate selves have diverted you from BEing One have had one thing in common. They share a purpose to keep you separate from BEing the light – your true power.

Surrender into the love that you are.
It is time to step into the pulse of life that inspires you
to the greatness of your BEing. Become the initiator
for higher insights, solutions, and brilliance in your
life, with others and in the world, by BEing you.

The warrioress, warrior, mother, father, child, mystic, singer, painter, visionary, wise one, truth sayer, angelic, writer, dancer, poet, leader, healer, builder, director, inventor, medicine woman, medicine man, dreamer, inspirer, wonder man, wonder woman, initiator, problem solver, birther, awakener and lover all live within you.

Our purest power waits to be found and transformed through our most hidden and forgotten soul parts.

The enlightenment that you seek is already within you.
The consciousness and wisdom within your
soul is meant to be your guide.

Opening to your soul aspects may unleash a sense of empowerment and vitality, but it may also bring up feelings like anxiety, fear, doubt and insecurity if you are in resistance of connecting to your truth and moving through your fears and controls.

Emotions when seen as gateways can reveal your spiritual path. They have the power to open your heart unlike anything else. When they come up you must remember that they are not "who you are," but are portals through what is unreal into what is most real within you. They can guide you onto the road of eternal wisdom, universal Oneness and will inevitably be the underlying impetus to help you create the change that catapults your life forward on the pathway of your highest soul expressions.

When you reconnect all of your soul fragments into the light within your body, then your True Self can be revealed. Your OverSoul or Higher Self – the "you" that oversees and guides you in every lifetime–can fully integrate back into your body and soul. You get to come home. Yet, for this to happen you must be willing to surrender completely in your Bodymind to the lessons and messages being given you.

You will know that you are hearing when you suspend your
need to snap to a conclusion about
a situation. You will know
that you are hearing when you are
connected to your breath in
your whole body and can feel your
feelings through your heart
and belly at the same time. You will
know that you are hearing
when you are surprised by the truths
coming out of your mouth,
and your life is rocked in the moment by the truth of Infinite
Source speaking through you.

The moment that you feel an aspect of your soul take root into your heart center and fill you with its essence, your life begins to align with your destiny.

Instead of *trying* to be all of the "wonderful" attributes of being spiritually awakened – embrace everything about you. Your humanness is your gateway. We live in very interesting times. We do not know how to be in touch with our humanness. We are afraid of letting go into our deepest vulnerabilities and fears. We are afraid of being found out as a fake and we project that onto others. We hold onto what makes us feel safe. Take responsibility for how terrified you are and beneath it all, you will find your True Self living in your soul and heart. Open to the reality that everything you need and seek lives within you. Embrace being vulnerable and honor your truth with that vulnerability.

Only love can heal you.

You are not your thoughts.
You are the spark of soul that lives within you.
God lives as Itself as your soul.
Seek God and love completely.
Love without regrets.

God is divine love and your choice to find union with love no matter how difficult your life circumstances, guides your way home through the veils and obstacles of illusion itself.

The enlightenment that you seek is already within you.
The consciousness and wisdom within your
soul is meant to be your guide.

When it comes to soul work and your spiritual truth, YOU cannot be found through a belief system. You can only be discovered through an authentic connection with all of yourself.

There is a difference between walking your own spiritual path and using "spirituality" as a way to manipulate your mind and emotions to get what you want in life. When you follow your true spiritual path, you may not get what you want, but you do get what you need.

You do not have to believe in anything to find your soul.
It will speak to you and guide you because it is YOU.

Deeper seeing integrates outer and inner sight. Outer sight is when your mind perceives what your physical eyesight can visualize. Inner sight allows you to begin to see the inner workings and energy of situations. Inner sight views the invisible energy that makes up individuals and relationships. Inner seeing allows you to see and BE with your Self. It allows you to embrace what is going on within you without fear. When you truly see what is "real," you are dual-seeing from the integration within your heart. When the two types of seeing are brought together through the heart, the truth of situations can be revealed.

You can begin a new way of seeing by looking into a part of your Self that is struggling. You will find a soul aspect waiting to be discovered within the darkness of your body. See through the darkness until you can sense the light hiding within this part of you. There is always light within darkness. Look for the light and see who is there and focus light from your heart into this aspect of you. You will find enormous wisdom and an immediate release of trapped emotions. Meet the inner fear and darkness with your compassion and love. Show up completely. As you see your own fear and choose to embrace it with love, then the love for yourself and others will grow. This is how you love yourself. This is how you truly learn to see.

A profound divine intelligence already exists within you waiting to be ignited and received.

Your true power is actually universal consciousness awakening as love. It is formed by reconnecting your Original and True Self with the consciousness of love and truth that you have known and experienced through hundreds or thousands of lifetimes.

No one can ever take away the freedom
that you find through your soul.

Whatever is needed to uplift and awaken your soul to make the connection into self-love and surrender and live in the simple truth of your heart will happen once you say "I am ready."

Excavate your inner most being for what is most arrogant, lost, disempowered and shut down and beneath it you will find the opening to your radiant light. Face the part of you that is afraid to come out and love it into presence and that is where you will find the next step to take for your life to flourish. Your soul, once reintegrated, finds its true strength. You become truth. You know what is real and what is not. Your soul knows what it needs. You are able to choose what to take with you and what to let go of.

The integration of love in your Bodymind creates a new power. However, unlike a power that is created through attachment, vanity, self-centeredness and greed, your new power will feel expansive and in-sync with the universe.

Becoming aware of *how* you have separated from your Original Self gives you the key to opening the door to your divine intelligence. The strength needed to open the door comes through clearing layers of your sanskaras (karmic impressions) and always choosing and following the love within you no matter how challenging. Love always takes you home. Always.

As the love within you begins to overflow, incredible joy and compassion for your life and for the world burst forth. As your heart opens, you may feel a surge of enormous emotion well up within your heart for the planet and for all of her inhabitants. Your truth will shine through your tears, blessing your life with healing, inspired action and relationships that bring you endless joys.

Whenever the light moves into the cellular level of the heart, mind and soul, suffering on a human level can be transformed into soul immersed universal understanding.

The truth of who you are is found by clearing the cellular memories within your body and choosing to see, feel and be in the divine truth of who you really are. Through the darkness is found the eternal blazing light that you are.

As you experience integrating and expressing your soul aspects into your Whole Self, remember that your greatest weaknesses are not in your soul. Your mind houses your greatest weaknesses when it is separate from Infinite Source. Each moment that your lower mind reacts from being separate from its God Mind, which is pure love, and believes its own stories, it creates a barrier or layer of disconnection within you. This separation to life creates a vault of emptiness, hatred and self-preservation and inhibits the free flow of light and love within you.

To heal your Core Wound requires suspending judgment and self-condemnation. Your wound can be healed when your heart can hold love for all of yourself, including your pain, grief, fear, resentment, or anger. It is so easy to get stuck and frozen in your emotions and to create your self-identity as your false Self. These emotions are not who you are, they are the feelings that are catalysts and portals of awakening into your True Self.

Your soul will communicate
with you through color, sound,
imagery, symbols, and words.
You will discover that your soul
has a language that is distinctively its own.
Your soul functions and communicates
to help you understand how your life purpose
and the world co-exist and co-create together.

Your soul is a bridge
between your mind and your emotions, your mind and
your body, and your mind and Spirit. It is an interpreter,
guide, healer, lover and innovator. Your soul is not just the
spark of your life; it is also the catalyst and gateway that
make it possible to BE ONE in yourself and with all of life.

The body and mind will align with the ego and all of its stories until you choose to identify with your God Self over your ego Self.

Light is the magnificence of love magnified
beyond what is imaginable.

The light unifies your life force, energy bodies
and higher universal mind, while integrating
the love and power of your soul.

Give over to the light everything that
you hold onto or cannot change.
Letting go is essential to live in self-forgiveness. By letting go, you give to Infinite Source your thoughts about yourself without judgment. You accept yourself for who you are in your body. As you release what holds you back and offer it over to Infinite Source, a channel of love and renewed faith and power is opened. When you give over to Infinite Source a difficulty in your life, Source gives you back a 360-degree perspective that empowers you to awaken.

When the mind loosens it attachments and grip on what it thinks it needs to exist, then the soul is able to embody its physical vehicle and begin to reconnect with Infinite Source.

Your soul is a fire of passion, clarity, determination, and peace that fuels the evolution of your BEing into its true destiny.

The fastest way to reunite the pure soul components of love and power within you is to reignite and reconnect your divine feminine and masculine soul aspects and energies.

Your love is a flame.
Your love is warm tender and roaring fire of
light communion with sacred truth. Who are
you within the borders of your heart?
Can you feel its essence burning, surging, touching, holding,
pushing away, sometimes fragile, listless, aching, wanting?
Can you know its flame? You are that.
All that you are is the golden embodied flame
of Oneness that exists within you.
BE within the earth of yourself, the water of your
well, the air of your breath, the fire of your passion
and the etheric expansion of your infinite nature.
May these elements give you serenity
and comfort and peace.

Each month when a woman begins her menstrual cycle she experiences the flow of life force, emotion, psychic energies and blood. Her womb expands into a cosmically tuned vessel of spiritual energy. The *First, Second* and *Third Power Point Center*s in women are gateways into divine power. A woman's womb is a vessel of infinitely powerful cosmic forces. A woman's womb holds the same consciousness and energies as mother earth. Rich, deep, tender, powerful, life giving, awakened, nourishing, gentle, creative, empowering, determined, succulent and ripe; a woman's womb feels the joys and pain of all life, because she carries the seed of life within her.

A woman not only feels her own connection to Infinite Source, but the feelings of others, and the entire universe. Her psyche, her subconscious, conscious mind and soul are in tune with the subtle forces of universal energies through her body because her hormones ignite brain patterns and perceptions that are constantly in relationship to the whole. When girls and women are supported to follow the rhythm and divine intelligence from within their wombs, they grow up with self-dignity and vision to heal and lead the world to live in divine order with natural law not man "made up" law. Harmony and fearless power are the natural state for a woman.

The essence of a woman's soul can be felt through the expansion of her sexuality whether through childbirth or higher octave lovemaking. A woman's soul is profoundly connected through her sexuality and as she opens to the light moving through her body, she can experience her divine essence. The reconnection to the divine feminine as flames of pure white fire from the earth's core has the power to ignite a woman's remembrance of her soul essence.

Our agreement to self-abandon, betray, and reject ourselves
is bred into us. We are taught to shove
aside our body rhythms,
inner voice, melodies, intuition, power,
creativity, truth, light,
and our knowingness. This counterproductive
behavior is fueled
by the social conformism and cultural norms of society,
expectations, and controls from
family and our own illusions
and ideas about who we think we should
be. At first blush, everything
we do seems to work to create comfort or safety. You
follow a certain behavior, action, or
belief because "that is the
way things work." It is how you believe
you will get what you need or want
most in this world.

A man must learn to work with the shifts in
his energies as much as a woman does.
Men also go through hormonal changes, but go through the full cycle of their hormonal peaks and valleys expressing in 24 hours. When a man ignores or denies his energetic cycles and works to control the impulses in his body or allows them to dominate him, he falls victim to his own powerlessness and this produces fear and his fear produces resistance in his body, mind and psyche. Resistance creates pain. When a man realizes how he controls the impulses and energy flows in his mind and body and instead of engaging with his ego to lead him through his life maze he engages his heart, a man begins his path of awakening.

A man discovers his soul essence through fully coming into his body on a feeling level and clearing all of the cords that block his connection to Infinite Source from the heart center down into his root center. A man must clear the energies that he takes on from his mother in utero and in early childhood and give her back all of the ways that he lives out her soul blueprint. Most women energetically transfer their emotional needs that are not being met by their partner on to their son. A boy grows into a man forging through his guilt, resentment, denial, despair and anger at his mother for emotionally bleeding him of his journey of becoming an expression of his True Self and taking back his power, rather than fulfilling her expectations she holds for him to be there for her. A woman's greatest gift to a boy or to a man is to not mother him to smother him. When a woman gives a man space to BE himself, she provides for him the opportunity to come through his spiritual pain created by his own past choices and past life karmas.

A man's spiritual pain evolves through the process of leaving himself, ignoring his feelings and energetic cycle's and by rejecting how the love within himself naturally wants to be expressed. A man's inner pain is created by building strong ego pathways that create behaviors that show others he is a capable man, one worth trusting by how he has built solid walls of denial to his Original Self. Boys are rarely taught how to love themselves, and are taught instead to get love through things, sex, false power and people. For a man to move through his spiritual pain he must first open his solar plexus and clear his root centers, and then find the womb of his life energies in his heart center. This will help him discover infinite love, his true essence. The life force powers of the earth and heavens meet in a man's heart and open the gateways to living in the transformative power of Spirit. His sexuality must reunite with his heart so that he can find his own connection to his divine feminine. His divine masculine will instantly transform as he receives and integrates the essence of his divine feminine power.

As a man unites his head, body and heart, he is able to permanently transform his relationship to his ego by entering into his eternal presence, his Original Self. A man must create a relationship of trust with his body and mind from a heart level. As he discovers and receives the love within his heart he can release his grip on control as a way to endure pain. He awakens to the ways that he has perpetuated inner pain and self-hatred, and as he embodies light, he can forgive himself and others in a profound way that brings peace to himself, others, and the world.

Your soul rejoining in love within your body ignites your spiritual power and creates the foundation of truth for you to ground your mind and heart. When your body and soul are aligned in Source power, your radiant light can shine forth, emanating power, joy and love. Your Original True Self is always present and ready to align the rest of you into its wholeness.

Feel your soul singing through your body.
BE willing to go beyond what your mind is saying and to love the essence of who you are, rather than what you think you are and what you have or do not have on the external.
Find the bliss of BEING the essence of *who you are.*

Your soul is you, the eternal child, wise elder, angel, creator, healer, lover and giver.

Keep letting go of your past, crumbling the walls of your ego, stepping into the expansiveness of your heart, and soaring with new wings.

We are all created equal in God's holy light and love. It is inevitable that as a global culture that the soul within every individual, regardless of the outer classification of nationality, race, sex, religion, creed or culture will be honored and supported to BE all that they are meant to BE. We are all destined to hear the call of our soul and to be given the opportunity to awaken to the deep presence and truth of our True Self during these times of light and dark struggle.

The power needed to uplift our world
and one another is found
only through love—
felt as authentic power.

In the new fractal matrix of Oneness, all dimensions of our awakening are experienced through pure consciousness – One light, love and power – without separation.

As your mind accepts the reality of your body and soul being unified, you have the opportunity to become synchronistic with time, space, and universal consciousness.

All of your lifetimes have been a dance with the polarities of light and dark—love and fear.
This dance moves you in and out of the state of Oneness.

Realize that your mind and body only split to the degree that you believe you are separate from Infinite Source.

All of us must become whole and One with our own hearts first, so that we can recognize how to be in relationship with life in a constructive way rather than blindly being destructive.

The peace that we create within our Bodymind
and soul can be gifted to the world in our
own unique and individualized ways.

Open to whatever God puts on your path with as much acceptance, love, and gratitude as you possibly can. Love yourself and let everything else be shown to you by grace itself.

At times, it takes enormous faith and trust to want to do the work to awaken. We fear losing what we have, yet what we have can not be compared to the joy of being a part of creating a shift in someone else's life and on the planet.

As your heart opens, you may feel a surge of enormous emotion well up within your heart for the planet and for all of her inhabitants. Your truth will shine through your tears, blessing your life with healing, inspired action and relationships that bring you endless joys. More important than anything else, you will feel the love in your heart and soul overflow into your body. Your body is the container for your True Self and bridges your soul with God in this dimension to accomplish your evolution in this lifetime.

Your Original Self is revealed through the process of restoring the light of your mind, heart and God unifying in your body. This reunion gives you the strength, courage and clarity to move through your biggest life challenges and to live your dreams by BEing who you are.

The light and love that live within you have the capacity to create union between your creativity, spirituality and physicality.

Your light propels you through the hurdles and obstacles that present themselves on your soul path. It reconnects your soul into the love within your body and reignites its full remembrance of that love.

The truth of who you are lives in the light that you are.

Light is the force of momentum that advances
your evolutionary process into Oneness.

When the light moves into the cellular level of the heart, mind and soul, suffering on a human level can be transformed into soul immersed universal understanding.

The truth of who you are is found by clearing the cellular memories within your body and choosing to see, feel and be in the divine truth of who you really are. Through the darkness is found the eternal blazing light that you are.

Your mind will always create "a story" that helps it to deal with the separations that it has created and wants to keep in place. It grasps onto anything and everything to rationalize its current state of existence, to be filled, and to feel safe and secure. Only when your mind has been guided by your higher Self to let go of its outer attachments and its perceptions can it begin to grasp the truth within your soul and feel the entryway into the God Body of breath and light that is within your physical and etheric energetic light grid.

If you sit in meditation or contemplation for a few minutes or for a few hours straight, or just take the time to be with yourself and become aware of your beliefs, you will discover how the mind and body habitually create conflict with one another. Their struggle to stand alone and separate from conscious connection with Infinite Source creates your suffering. The body and mind will align with the ego and all of its stories until you choose to identify with your God Self over your ego Self.

By engaging the channel of light from your solar plexus down into your root center a veil is removed from your mind and a gateway is opened into a deeper power. When you connect the light streaming from your solar plexus into your root center a portal of well-being opens that increases the strength of your core Self.

Your soul is always speaking the language of light and will guide you to awaken. As the light is ignited in all of your cells a new DNA of joy, vision and clarity can be birthed.

To strengthen your connection to finding and living in your soul purpose, take a moment to connect into your Creation Point. As a reminder your Creation Point is about 2.5 inches directly below your navel. Bring your awareness into your Creation Point and breathe 5 long inhalations and exhalations that move into the lumbar vertebras (your lower spine vertebras directly across from your Creation Point.) Drop your mind into your Creation Point and let go of your thinking mind. Feel your lower back growing wider as you breathe long and deep. BE with the energies of your Creation Point and meditate into your breath, allowing the flow of divine grace and wisdom to move into all of the cells in your body.

As you "think" from your Creation Point, you will be able to follow a greater power of life force energy that can open the direction of your life to new possibilities and strengthen your connection to your higher wisdom. Fulfilling your soul's calling may mean you have to shift how you think, where you live, who you work for, who you live with, or what you eat.

Your soul will give you the ingredients to recreate your life no matter where you presently find yourself.

The ultimate key to your breakthroughs and success emanates from where you come from in yourself, when and how you ask yourself your inner questions, and how you show up to serve Infinite Source in your daily activities.

To feel deeply, your emotional heart must feel safe. Placing your attention in your solar plexus and sitting in a golden and warm pool of light creates the foundation to opening into feeling. Your heart center can relax, and your solar plexus and your mind can merge, opening up pathways of light into your soul.

Whether you are planting a garden, creating a salad, fixing a roof, painting on a canvas, writing a new corporate or political policy, changing a diaper, sitting at your computer, being on social media, cooking dinner, or doing the laundry – pay attention to BEing One in your Self, and One with your heart.

Enter into the light within yourself. Place your focus into the core shaft of light that surrounds your spine. Breathe into the light within your core shaft. Let it BE your foundation of support to live life from. Choose the light over following the roller coaster ride of your thoughts. Choose the light over your thoughts and stories about yourself and others.

BE aware of where and how you split off from your Self. BE aware of what you think about or continuously obsess over. When you split off into following a random thought in your mind, bring yourself back to the light within your heart center. Then, reconnect your focus from your heart center with the light within your solar plexus, Creation Point, lower belly, and root center. You grow and expand where your attention goes. Where you focus your attention opens the gateway into your truth. BE present with your intention. What do you want to create? Joy, peace, love, bliss, true abundance on all levels, trust, courage, fulfillment, contribution, fearlessness, leadership, innovation, truth? What attribute vibrates your wholeness and full sense of Self?

Commit to let go of anything that is a diversion to what you really want to create. As you align into the light and release your mind, you can fully align into Oneness.

Understand how you separate the dark and light in your body and psyche and learn to embrace the dark within yourself and find the light within the dark to transmute your energies into whole consciousness.

As the light increases within you, your ego is unable
to maintain its grip, your mind becomes unable
to live from fear and your heart becomes unable
to stay closed. Living in union bridges light and
dark and cracks through your veils of illusion.

As you connect into the light and unite your mind and body, you will be able to move through dualism—the split between what you think is real and what actually is.

When you follow the light within, it supports you to end how you energetically repress your spiritual power and helps give birth to a new power within you. Your new power is formed as you reconnect the light of your soul with the light of Infinite Source.

The old power matrix within you will hold on to thinking and doing things to keep you in a comfort zone and in control. It will work hard to have you stay subservient to its arrogance and seductions. Realize that your old power lives as fear within your body. It was originally created by your ego as a way for your unrealized soul aspects to survive. Your soul aspects and ego have only known how to function through reactivity and control. Your soul reconnection with the light changes that dynamic. Light can and will clear whatever you choose for it to clear.

Give over to the light everything that you hold onto or cannot change. Letting go is essential to live in self-forgiveness. By letting go, you give to Infinite Source your thoughts about yourself without judgment. You accept yourself for who you are in your body. As you release what holds you back and offer it over to Infinite Source, a channel of love and renewed faith and power is opened. When you give over to Infinite Source a difficulty in your life, Source gives you back a 360-degree perspective that empowers you to awaken. It is through facing your life challenges with love and self-forgiveness that a deeper relationship with Infinite Source is created.

As you love the holiness within you,
You will be able to forgive yourself,
Have compassion for yourself and others,
Trust yourself and God.
As you love yourself,
You will find,
The light of God BEing
Itself as You.

The light awakening in your body cracks open the truth of who you are. When you follow the light within, it supports you to end how you energetically repress your spiritual power and helps give birth to a new power within you.

By inviting into your body, and especially into your solar plexus and heart centers, the penetrating white and gold light of Infinite Source, you will clear the old power that fuels your fear and blockages, and keeps you "walled in and small." By asking the universe for guidance from your heart center—the heart of your soul, you will always be led in the perfect direction of your life.

The difficulties and challenges that come up in your life are meant to be teachers; things you learn from and then let go of. As you welcome, accept and surrender to the infinite love that is the divine expression of you and Infinite Source in union, the unique qualities of your light can manifest in every area of your life.

As your ego mind lets go and surrenders to "running the show of your life" and instead follows how the love within your soul leads you, you will come through the battles between your mind and soul.

When you follow the voice of your truth,
your ego Self cannot hold on.

All war, poverty and issues of violence are created from battling the two polar forces of love and power, our divine masculine and feminine, up against one another.

When we split off from our spiritual power
we align with the emptiness within our being,
which is experienced as the dark.

Awakening into the light that you are opens you to Oneness consciousness.

Your divine truth—your soul essence—is the nectar of healing and rejuvenation in every cell of your body. The universe and you become One as the molecules of thoughts, feelings, and energies emerge and blossom from the seeds of your soul. There is no going back once you walk through the doorway of your heart.

Open to whatever God puts on your path
with as much acceptance, love, and
gratitude as you possibly can.
Love yourself and let everything else be
shown to you by grace itself.

Integrating your soul reveals the roadmap of your life.
It is not a belief system. It is a direct experience.

To live fearlessly requires only one thing,
complete trust in the light that you are.

In the last moments of life,
people don't think about the money they have or don't have.
They think about love and who has touched their lives.
In the beginning all there is love.
In the end, love is all there is.
In between the two, you are given the opportunity
to know the true wealth of love and the
hidden codes into eternal happiness.
When you choose the love in your Self,
you can finally heal and BE free.

When you are One in Soul – you become love.

BE in the silence, the stillness, the movement,
the song and the joy within your heart.

Love and power are our birthright as human beings. Yet we have been trained to separate love and power for centuries. By separating these two vital energies we have created the dynamics of pain and suffering in our lives and in the systems of the world.

The sorrow and suffering that we all encounter at some point in our lives are gateways into our next level of enlightening. Never forget that they are given from the divine to help us become One and whole.

The heart of your soul knows love because it is love.

Live BEing the love that you are and experience the miracle of your existence.

Life wants to give you the keys to the
great mystery within you.

Light is the force of momentum that advances
your evolutionary unfoldment into Oneness.

Your heart center, which is your true mind, is like a tuning fork that resonates to the thoughts and feelings of the universe. It is the entry way into unlimited consciousness and infinite awareness.

The truth of who you are is found by clearing the cellular memories within your body and choosing to see, feel, and BE in the divine truth of who you really are. Through the darkness within you, the eternal blazing light that you are is found.

Each time that you choose courage, fearlessness, determination, love, and compassion, know that someone else is benefitting by your choice. You can be sure that someone will feel it. We are all linked together by a golden light grid of love. The more of us that do this, the more we can help to shift the vibrations around the globe.

When we become One and whole with our own hearts,
only then can we hear and feel the earth and serve
her by becoming an instrument of love and peace
in our own lives, with others and in the world.

Imagine for a moment resolving your inner battles within your Self for the benefit of all beings. Imagine ending the wars within you, and creating peace within your Self. Can you embrace for a moment how powerful it would be to express peace in your life rather than your unresolved inner wars? We live in a world of duality, and all of us have the challenge of ending our attachments to how our mind controls through creating, and reacting to fear. As you become *One in Soul*, you have the opportunity and new momentum to discover, and implement new ways of leading, serving, and uplifting humanity.

When enough of us shift out of the frequency of separation and inner battle, we can create, and implement new approaches, and models for business, finance, the arts, education, politics, social justice, leadership and global unity. Rather than leading through hate, separation, fear, and ego, humanity can step through the veils of sorrow created through soul separation into soul oneness.

May the light be revealed that is in your heart and uplift your life to BE all that you know it can BE.

As you activate the energies and intelligence of your soul aspects through your heart, you will discover the emergence of divine love. The heart of your soul knows love because it is love. It is the only activation of life that can free you.

Love is the root.
Love is the true power.
It is the foundation of all things.

Continually choose to build the stability created within your relationship to your soul. This anchor will give you the courage to enter through the higher energies and more advanced doorways of Spirit.

No one can ever take away the freedom that you
find through your soul. Whatever is needed to uplift
and awaken your soul to make the connections
into self-love and surrender and live in the simple
truth of your heart will happen once you say,
"I am ready."

Hold the space of unconditional love and support from your whole heart for your journey and for those around you.

The enlightenment that you seek is already within you.

Each time that you allow greater light to come into your Whole Self, you create a momentum to evolve and move forward.

Once you are connected to your soul's truth in your body, the next levels of realization, integration, and alignment in Infinite Source can occur. Your soul is always speaking the language of light and will guide you to awaken. As the light is ignited in all of your cells, a new DNA of joy, vision, and clarity can be birthed.

Breakthrough the silence
Breakthrough the pain
Let go of wondering what there's to gain,
The final frontier is in the receiving
The release of the me,
Into thee.

May these *One in Soul Imprints* bring to you moments of sweet realization and the release from all suffering.

Iana Lahi

Enjoy these blank pages to imprint
the messages of your heart.

www.ingramcontent.com/pod-product-compliance
Lightning Source LLC
Chambersburg PA
CBHW031415290426
44110CB00011B/384